THINKATHON 2

written by Charlotte S. Jaffe
and Barbara T. Roberts

895

97.2.6

E. Doyle

EDUCATIONAL
IMPRESSIONS

ISBN 0-910857-08-3

EDUCATIONAL IMPRESSIONS, INC.
Hawthorne, New Jersey 07507

Cover Design and Illustrations by Emilie Doyle

CONTENTS

THINKATHON II

OVERVIEW

Thinkathon is an exciting contest that challenges the students' higher level thinking skills and offers the teachers an excellent evaluation tool! The book is divided into six activity sections: HYPOTHESIZING, WHICH ONE DOES NOT BELONG?, MAKING COMPARISONS, TRIVIA, MATH AND LOGIC QUIZ, AND LANGUAGE PUZZLERS.

DIRECTIONS

Thinkathon can be used within one classroom, between classrooms or schools, or among several school districts.

1. TEAMS

   The students are divided into teams of equal number. Each team member is given a creative name tag (flower, animal, book, etc.) which represents the team name. (Students may design their own.) Each team rotates through six activities. The team's total score is compiled at the end of these activities.

2. ACTIVITIES

   Each activity is conducted by a group leader for approximately fifteen minutes. Two minutes should be allowed for direction and thirteen minutes for skill involvement. Each activity should be held in a separate area of the classroom or school so that the element of surprise will be the same for each team. Each activity page in this book is designed for a fifteen minute period; however, the teacher may choose to change the time structure and use more than one activity per contest. Activity pages not used in the contest may be used as practice pages. There is diversity in the degree of difficulty. Easier activities are found in the beginning of each section.

3. SCORING

   The first page of each activity section contains directions
for scoring. Activities may be scored as team or individual
efforts. If a team effort is used, the group leader may choose
to record the team's answers on the board as team members call
them out and total them at the end of the time limit. One point
is awarded for each correct team answer. If an individual effort
is used, one point is awarded for each correct answer on each
team member's activity sheet.

4. CONCLUSION

   At the conclusion of the contest, all team members assemble
in one location for the awarding of the certificates of partic-
ipation and certificates of special merit (to the winners).
These awards may be duplicated from the models in the book.

                                    Charlotte S. Jaffe

                                    Barbara T. Roberts

SECTION I

HYPOTHESIZING

Suggested Time: 15 minutes

(2 minutes for directions)

(13 minutes for competitive activity)

In this section, students are asked to respond to a hypothetical situation and list their responses at the bottom of each page.

EXAMPLE: Why was the school bus late?
1. Bus driver overslept
2. Bus had a flat tire

There may be a wide variety of acceptable answers in this section. When time is up, total points on each team member's activity page. Example: 12 correct answers = 12 points. If the activity is conducted as a team effort and answers are recorded on the blackboard, the scoring is one point for each correct answer. Tally each team's total and record it on the scoresheet next to the team name.

HYPOTHESIZING

Andrew waited on the corner for his school bus to arrive. Ten minutes passed, then twenty more! Finally, the school bus appeared. "Why were you late?" Andrew asked the weary bus driver. What was her reply? List your ideas in the space below. Number each response.

What is happening in the scene below? Be sure to consider
unusual possibilities! List your ideas on the bottom half of
the page and number your responses.

HYPOTHESIZING

A crowd of people gathered on the corner of Maple and Main Streets. What brought them there? List your ideas in the space below. Number each response.

HYPOTHESIZING

Steve and Pete had looked forward to a swim in the cool
stream. It had been a hot day and they had hiked for many hours.
To their dismay, they discovered that the Health Department had
posted a sign, warning that the stream was unsafe for swimming
or drinking. What do you think had caused the problem? Write
your ideas in the space below and number your responses.

HYPOTHESIZING

The three plants pictured below were started at the same time. Why did plant three grow faster than the other two? Stretch your mind to think of unusual reasons! List your ideas in the space below and number each response.

HYPOTHESIZING

Billy was very disappointed when he received a poor grade on his history test. What might have caused his problem? List your ideas in the space below and number your responses!

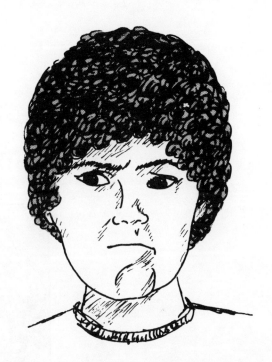

HYPOTHESIZING

Elizabeth is overjoyed! In fact, she's been saying all day that it's the happiest day of her life! What do you suppose might explain Elizabeth's mood? List your answers below and number them.

HYPOTHESIZING

Carol's mother arrived home from work late in the after-
noon. When she opened the door of her teen-aged daughter's room,
she was greeted by an unpleasant sight. "What a mess!" she
exclaimed. "I wonder what happened here?" Write your ideas in
the space below. Be sure to number your responses.

HYPOTHESIZING

What is happening in the picture below? What reasons can you suggest to explain why this boy is shouting? List your ideas on this page and number your answers.

HYPOTHESIZING

Members of a scout troop agreed to meet at 9:00 A.M. at the lake for a clean-up activity. Dan was there at 9:00 but none of the others came. He waited for 30 minutes. No one else arrived so he went home. What happened? What are some possible explanations for Dan's situation? Number your answers.

HYPOTHESIZING

A person known for lifelong thriftiness suddenly begins spending money freely. How can you explain this change in behavior? How many responses can you make? Number your answers as you list them below. Use your imagination!

HYPOTHESIZING

Welcome to the world of the future! It is the year 2120. Life is quite different on our planet. People do not read books anymore. Libraries have been closed. What has caused this to happen? List your ideas in the space below and number your responses.

SECTION II

WHICH ONE DOES NOT BELONG?

Suggested Time: 15 minutes

(2 minutes for directions)

(13 minutes for competitive activity)

The activity pages in this section contain sets of four words. In each set of 4, 3 of the items share something in common. Students are asked to recognize the one which doesn't share the commonality. Each page is designed to be used in a 13 minute time limit; however, depending on the ability level, you may wish to use more than one page in the time allotted. When the time limit has expired, total the correct answers on each team member's page. Example: 15 correct responses = 15 points. Tally each team's total and record it on the score-sheet next to the team name. If the activity is conducted as a team effort and answers are recorded on the blackboard, the scoring is also one point for each correct answer.

It is possible that some students may choose different answers from the ones given in the answer sheet. If their reasons are valid, they should receive credit for a correct response.

WHICH ONE DOES NOT BELONG?

Circle the correct answer.

1. Blue	Purple	Red	Yellow
2. Mercury	Venus	Earth	Mars
3. Zebra	Skunk	Chipmunk	Leopard
4. Fez	Beret	Turban	Caftan
5. Baseball	Tennis	Soccer	Croquet
6. U.S.A.	England	Canada	Australia
7. Laser	Camera	Microphone	Microscope
8. Avocado	Apple	Grape	Coconut
9. Snail	Egg	Walnut	Pretzel
10. 14	49	35	58
11. Blazer	Vest	Cardigan	Windbreaker
12. Mexico	Zanzibar	Cuba	Bermuda
13. Pound	Peso	Rouble	Lyre
14. Tampa	Tallahassee	Orlando	Macon
15. Montreal	Mexico City	Denver	Rio de Janeiro

WHICH ONE DOES NOT BELONG?

Circle the correct answer.

1. Starfish	Clam	Snake	Crab
2. Coat	Shoe	Blouse	Vest
3. Spring	Autumn	Christmas	Summer
4. Snow	Rain	Hail	Sun
5. Den	Porch	Kitchen	Bedroom
6. Baseball	Wrestling	Football	Hockey
7. Canoe	Submarine	Sailboat	Motorboat
8. Pond	Lake	Valley	River
9. Book	Pencil	Pen	Crayon
10. Chair	Iron	Refrigerator	Lamp
11. Nail	Hammmer	Wrench	Screwdriver
12. Mickey Mouse	Donald Duck	Bambi	Lassie
13. One	Four	Three	Seven
14. Baltimore	Colorado	Connecticut	Ohio
15. Coin	Ball	Kite	Dish

WHICH ONE DOES NOT BELONG?

Circle the correst answer.

1.	Ash	Elm	Aspen	Peony
2.	Marigold	Pansy	Rose	Petunia
3.	24	38	16	56
4.	Pentagon	Rectangle	Triangle	Oval
5.	Barracuda	Aleutian	Piranha	Mackerel
6.	Koala	Beaver	Opossum	Kangaroo
7.	Manx	Spaniel	Tabby	Calico
8.	Penguin	Pelican	Ostrich	Rhea
9.	Goalie	Catcher	Shortstop	Pitcher
10.	Mocassin	Loafer	Oxford	Stetson
11.	Button	Snap	Key	Zipper
12.	Calf	Kitten	Pony	Foal
13.	21	15	27	19
14.	Scarlet	Beige	Ruby	Crimson
15.	Accelerator	Clutch	Piston	Parquet

WHICH ONE DOES NOT BELONG?

Circle the correct answer.

1. Mahogany	Ebony	Cedar	Flax
2. Nylon	Cotton	Dacron	Rayon
3. Sundial	Clock	Thermometer	Calendar
4. Brick	Blood	Lemon	Rose
5. Rubber	Sap	Gum	Mint
6. Texas	Massachusetts	Virginia	Pennsylvania
7. Japan	Iceland	Italy	Philippines
8. 28	68	30	72
9. Daisy	Rose	Iris	Bluebell
10. Parchesi	Poker	Monopoly	Checkers
11. Nylon	Wool	Linen	Silk
12. Pane	Two	Last	Maid
13. Sneezy	Vanity	Happy	Sleepy
14. Queen	Worker	Drone	Monarch
15. 40	22	13	15

WHICH ONE DOES NOT BELONG?

Circle the correct answer.

1. Willie Mays	Red Grange	Joe Namath	O.J. Simpson
2. Franklin Stove	Bifocal Lens	Harmonica	Telegraph
3. Bald Eagle	Whooping Crane	Herring Gull	Blue Whale
4. 28	36	16	22
5. Cherry	Cloud	Blood	Valentine
6. Femur	Ulna	Tibia	Fibula
7. Japan	China	Korea	Spain
8. Mussels	Oysters	Crabs	Clams
9. Robert Peary	Ronald Amundsen	Richard Byrd	John Cabot
10. Thyroid	Adrenal	Pituitary	Kidney
11. Suspension	Superior	Draw	Cantilever
12. COBOL	BASIC	NASA	FORTRAN
13. Harvard	Hoover	Princeton	Yale
14. Great Dane	Chihuahua	Pomeranian	Yorkshire Terrier
15. Surrealism	Cubism	Impressionism	Communism

WHICH ONE DOES NOT BELONG?

Circle the correct answer.

1. Memorial   Arbor   Labor   Urban

2. Flat   Hook   Sharp   Earth

3. Vulture   Hawk   Pigeon   Osprey

4. Ravioli   Spaghetti   Lasagne   Zucchini

5. Okra   Zinnia   Aster   Pansy

6. Diplodocus   Tyrannosaurus   Brontosaurus   Brachiosaurus

7. Tugboat   Sloop   Xebec   Galley

8. Ocelot   Giraffe   Leopard   Elephant

9. Golf club   Baseball bat   Bowling pin   Tennis racquet

10. Pole vault   Pommel horse   Balance beam   Parallel bars

11. Lake Superior Lake Placid   Lake Erie   Lake Huron

12. Monkey   Roadrunner   Cactus   Yucca

13. Gothic   Siberian   Romanesque   Victorian

14. Walrus   Polar bear   Yak   Collared lemming

15. Cub   Puppy   Fawn   Stallion

WHICH ONE DOES NOT BELONG?

Circle the correct answer.

1. Measure	Mean	Sharp	Flat
2. Necklace	Bracelet	Button	Earring
3. Cheese	Juice	Butter	Milk
4. Blade	Mogul	Slalom	Snowplow
5. Float	Tango	Waltz	Minuet
6. Rummy	Bridge	Monopoly	Canasta
7. Coffee pot	Tea kettle	Spatula	Pitcher
8. Polo	Bit	Bridle	Reins
9. Baritone	Octave	Tenor	Soprano
10. Wheat	Rice	Barley	Potato
11. Inch	Centimeter	Millimeter	Kilometer
12. Under	Open	Above	Over
13. Bell	Flashlight	Candle	Lamp
14. Fox	Sheep	Cow	Horse
15. Reject	Decline	Refuse	Choose

WHICH ONE DOES NOT BELONG?

Circle the Correct Answer

1. Quartets   Triplets   Quintuplets   Twins

2. Harpsichord   Cello   Oboe   Guitar

3. 21   15   7   14

4. Bonnet   Beret   Cuff   Cap

5. Zaire   Taiwan   Kenya   Zambia

6. Uranus   Moon   Saturn   Earth

7. 24   60   15   39

8. Python   Rattlesnake   Cobra   Copperhead

9. Eleanor Roosevelt Thomas Jefferson John Kennedy   Susan B. Anthony

10. Franc   Hectare   Mark   Dollar

11. 12   42   53   18

12. Anatomy   Biology   History   Chemistry

13. Mare   Ewe   Stallion   Doe

14. Jump   Swim   Jogger   Laugh

15. Garage   Barn   Stable   Coop

WHICH ONE DOES NOT BELONG?

Circle the correct answer.

1. Barometer   Speedometer   Thermometer   Anemometer

2. Gazelle   Cheetah   Greyhound   Turtle

3. Lincoln   Coolidge   Stevenson   Johnson

4. Australia   Asia   North America   United Kingdom

5. Cow   Dog   Cat   Gerbil

6. Scorpio   Virgo   Leo   Horatio

7. Vacuum cleaner   Broom   Dishwasher   Washing machine

8. Filly   Colt   Doe   Mare

9. Babe Ruth   Ty Cobb   Wilt Chamberlain   Joe DiMaggio

10. Chile   Brazil   Peru   Argentina

11. Dickens   Picasso   Miró   Rembrandt

12. Private   Colonel   Sergeant   Admiral

13. Aruba   Puerto Rico   Bermuda   Costa Rica

14. Niña   Mayflower   Pinta   Santa Maria

15. Robert E. Lee   Patrick Henry   Samuel Adams   Benjamin Franklin

WHICH ONE DOES NOT BELONG?

Circle the correct answer.

1. Strawberry	Peach	Pear	Apple
2. Koala	Kangaroo	Lion	Dingo
3. James Monroe	James Madison	Patrick Henry	Thomas Jefferson
4. Mango	Lime	Orange	Lemon
5. Mississippi	Missouri	Nile	Amazon
6. Mosque	Temple	Cathedral	Adobe
7. Silver	Lead	Gold	Platinum
8. Prison	Slalom	Penitentiary	Dungeon
9. Aphid	Mosquito	Anemone	Gnat
10. Owl	Hawk	Falcon	Cardinal
11. Whales	Frogs	Ducks	Butterflies
12. Canasta	Pinochle	Rummy	Backgammon
13. Wombat	Griffin	Unicorn	Pegasus
14. Cabbage	Spinach	Beans	Lettuce
15. Iroquois	Inca	Navaho	Cherokee

WHICH ONE DOES NOT BELONG?

Circle the correct answer.

1. Clam	Oyster	Scallop	Crab
2. Tortoise	Frog	Lizard	Snake
3. Spider	Cricket	Ladybug	Locust
4. Scorpion	Water Moccasin	Dragonfly	Gila Monster
5. Trenton	Baltimore	Denver	Sacramento
6. Corvette	Dodge	Ford	Buick
7. Lumber	Paper	Pulp	Ink
8. Krypton	Electron	Proton	Neutron
9. Ice cream	Cotton Candy	Lemon	Honey
10. Blimp	Kite	Glider	Parachute
11. Lion	Great White Shark	Screech Owl	Quail
12. Whale	Dolphin	Seal	Eel
13. Curtain	Carpet	Rug	Tile
14. Meter	Liter	Ounce	Gram
15. Gills	Fins	Scales	Lungs

WHICH ONE DOES NOT BELONG?

Circle the correct answer.

1. Capillary   Vein   Artery   Ligament

2. Egypt   Sudan   Algeria   Iraq

3. 15   24   41   36

4. Virgo   Andromeda   Gemini   Taurus

5. Tiara   Necklace   Brooch   Damask

6. Squirrel   Rabbit   Hamster   Monkey

7. Ginger   Cinnamon   Nutmeg   Parsley

8. Celery   Turnip   Potato   Carrot

9. Congress   Presidency FBI   Senate

10. Osprey   Skiff   Dinghy   Sloop

11. Lemon   Lime   Avocado   Artichoke

12. Margin   Border   Interior   Perimeter

13. Volt   Watt   Mph   Amp

14. Tsunamis   Pyrenees   Himalayas   Dolomites

15. Picasso   Casals   Monet   Wyeth

WHICH ONE DOES NOT BELONG?

ANSWERS

NB-1

1. Purple
2. Earth
3. Leopard
4. Caftan
5. Soccer
6. Australia
7. Microphone
8. Coconut
9. Pretzel
10. 58
11. Vest
12. Mexico
13. Lyre
14. Macon
15. Rio de Janeiro

NB-2

1. Snake
2. Shoe
3. Christmas
4. Sun
5. Porch
6. Wrestling
7. Submarine
8. Valley
9. Book
10. Chair
11. Nail
12. Lassie
13. Four
14. Baltimore
15. Kite

NB-3

1. Peony
2. Rose
3. 38
4. Oval
5. Aleutian
6. Beaver
7. Spaniel
8. Pelican
9. Goalie
10. Stetson
11. Key
12. Pony
13. 19
14. Beige
15. Parquet

NB-4

1. Flax
2. Cotton
3. Thermometer
4. Lemon
5. Mint
6. Texas
7. Italy
8. 30
9. Bluebell
10. Poker
11. Nylon
12. Last
13. Vanity
14. Monarch
15. 15

NB-5

1. Willie Mays
2. Telegraph
3. Herring Gull
4. 22
5. Cloud
6. Ulna
7. Spain
8. Crabs
9. John Cabot
10. Kidney
11. Superior
12. NASA
13. Hoover
14. Great Dane
15. Communism

NB-6

1. Urban
2. Sharp
3. Pigeon
4. Zucchini
5. Okra
6. Tyrannosaurus
7. Tugboat
8. Elephant
9. Bowling pin
10. Pole vault
11. Lake Placid
12. Monkey
13. Siberian
14. Yak
15. Stallion

WHICH ONE DOES NOT BELONG?

ANSWERS

NB-7

1. Mean
2. Button
3. Juice
4. Blade
5. Float
6. Monopoly
7. Spatula
8. Polo
9. Octave
10. Potato
11. Inch
12. Open
13. Bell
14. Fox
15. Choose

NB-8

1. Quartets
2. Oboe
3. 15
4. Cuff
5. Taiwan
6. Moon
7. 39
8. Python
9. Eleanor Roosevelt
10. Hectare
11. 53
12. History
13. Stallion
14. Jogger
15. Garage

NB-9

1. Speedometer
2. Turtle
3. Stevenson
4. United Kingdom
5. Cow
6. Horatio
7. Broom
8. Doe
9. Wilt Chamberlain
10. Brazil
11. Dickens
12. Admiral
13. Costa Rica
14. Mayflower
15. Robert E. Lee

NB-10

1. Strawberry
2. Lion
3. Patrick Henry
4. Mango
5. Nile
6. Adobe
7. Lead
8. Slalom
9. Anemone
10. Cardinal
11. Butterflies
12. Backgammon
13. Wombat
14. Beans
15. Inca

NB-11

1. Crab
2. Frog
3. Spider
4. Dragonfly
5. Baltimore
6. Corvette
7. Ink
8. Krypton
9. Lemon
10. Blimp
11. Quail
12. Eel
13. Curtain
14. Ounce
15. Lungs

NB-12

1. Ligament
2. Iraq
3. 41
4. Andromeda
5. Damask
6. Monkey
7. Parsley
8. Celery
9. FBI
10. Osprey
11. Lemon
12. Interior
13. Mph
14. Tsunamis
15. Casals

MAKING COMPARISONS

On each page of this activity section, students are asked to compare two subjects. They must list their responses according to similarities and differences.

Example: Compare and contrast an airplane and a train.

ALIKE

1.   Both are means of transportation

DIFFERENT

Plane

1.   Plane travels in air

Train

1.   Train travels on ground

There may be a wide variety of acceptable answers in this section. SCORING: When time is up, total the points on each team member's activity page. Example: 12 correct answers = 12 points. If the activity is conducted as a team effort and answers are recorded on the blackboard, the scoring is one point for each correct answer. Tally each team's total and record it on the score-sheet next to the team name.

MAKING COMPARISONS

How are a train and an airplane alike? How are they different?
Compare and contrast these two means of transportation. List your
answers in the space below. Be sure to number your responses!

ALIKE

DIFFERENT

Train   Plane

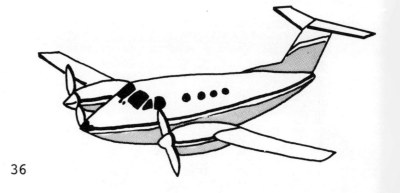

36

MAKING COMPARISONS

How are a monkey and a tiger alike? How are they different?
Compare the ways and list your answers in the spaces below. Number each response.

ALIKE

DIFFERENT

Monkey   Tiger

37

MAKING COMPARISONS

How are a computer and a telephone alike? How are they different? List the ways in the spaces below and number your responses.
Stretch your mind to think of unusual responses!

ALIKE

DIFFERENT

Computer   Telephone

38

MAKING COMPARISONS

How are a clock and a calendar alike? How are they different?
List the ways in the spaces below and number your responses.
Stretch your mind to think of unusual responses!

ALIKE

DIFFERENT

Clock   Calendar

MAKING COMPARISONS

How are the igloo and the island house alike? How are they different? It's fun to contrast and compare these two unusual types of shelter! List your answers in the spaces below and number your responses.

ALIKE

DIFFERENT

Igloo   Island House

40

MAKING COMPARISONS

How are the sports of basketball and soccer alike? How are they different? Compare and contrast these two popular sports! List your answers in the spaces below. Be sure to number your responses.

<u>ALIKE</u>

<u>DIFFERENT</u>

<u>Basketball</u>   <u>Soccer</u>

MAKING COMPARISONS

How are a teddy bear and a doll alike? How are they different? List the ways in the spaces below and number your responses. Think hard and try to find some unusual responses!

ALIKE

DIFFERENT

Teddy Bear   Doll

MAKING COMPARISONS

How is an artist like an author? How are they different?
Stretch your mind to compare and contrast the two occupations!
List your answers in the spaces below. Be sure to number your
responses.

ALIKE

DIFFERENT

Artist   Author

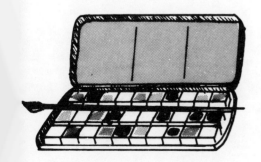

MAKING COMPARISONS

How are a whale and a gold fish alike? How are they different? List the ways in the spaces below and number your answers. Try to think of as many responses as you can!

ALIKE

DIFFERENT

Whale   Gold Fish

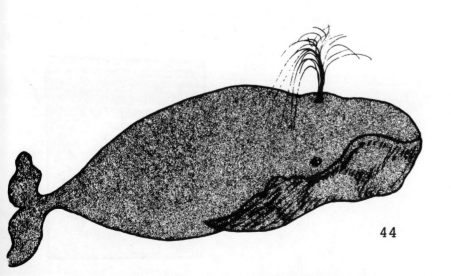

MAKING COMPARISONS

How are a camera and an eye alike? How are they different?
Number your answers as you list them in the spaces below. Try to
think of some unusual responses.

ALIKE

DIFFERENT

Camera   Eye

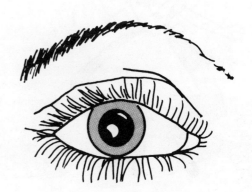

MAKING COMPARISONS

Consider two popular storybook characters, Alice In Wonderland and Dorothy in The Wizard of Oz. How are they alike? How are they different? List your ideas in the spaces below. Be sure to number your responses.

<u>ALIKE</u>

<u>DIFFERENT</u>

<u>Alice</u>   <u>Dorothy</u>

MAKING COMPARISONS

How are Christopher Columbus and Neil Armstrong alike? How are they different? List the ways in the space below and number your responses. Stretch your mind to think of unusual responses!

ALIKE

DIFFERENT

Christopher Columbus   Neil Armstrong

TRIVIA

Suggested Time: 15 minutes

(2 minutes for directions)

(13 minutes for competitive activity)

In this activity section, students are asked to respond to a variety of general knowledge questions. In the case of two-part answers, both parts must be correct in order to score a point. Although each contest is composed of twenty-four questions, the teacher may decide to use the number of questions suitable to the group's ability. Scoring: When time is up, total the number of points on each team member's activity page. If the activity is conducted as a team effort and the answers are recorded on the blackboard, the scoring is one point for each correct team answer. Tally each team's total and record it on the scoresheet next to the team name.

TRIVIA

1. What American city is known as "The City of Brotherly Love"?

2. As a colony, this state was named for a king of England.

3. What is the usual temperature of a healthy person?

4. What king was the ruler of Camelot?

5. This Boston silversmith is famous for a patriotic midnight ride during the Revolutionary War.

6. This filmmaker has given us E.T., Close Encounters of the Third Kind and Raiders of the Lost Ark.

7. This term is used to refer to the process by which a tadpole becomes a frog.

8. This chemical helps prevent tooth decay.

9. Steve Carlton is associated with what sport?

10. In what sport will you use the term "slap shot"?

11. Among other paintings, he painted "The Last Supper."

12. One of her most famous books is Little House on the Prairie.

TRIVIA

13. This country has the largest population in the world. Its capital is Peking.

14. This game of skill is played with bishops, knights, kings, and queens.

15. Who was the legendary outlaw of Sherwood Forest?

16. In the nursery rhyme "Old King Cole" how many fiddlers did the king have?

17. How many sides does an octagon have?

18. These brothers flew their first airplane at Kitty Hawk, North Carolina, in 1903.

19. What number does the following Roman numeral represent?

     XIV = _____

20. In which state will you find "The Alamo"?

21. In the story of "Jack and the Beanstalk," what musical instrument did Jack take from the giant?

22. Name the woman who is credited with being the designer of the first American flag.

23. Julius Erving is an outstanding player in this sport.

24. Name the melted rock that flows from a volcano.

TRIVIA

1. The Smithsonian Institute is located in this city.

2. In which state will you find Mount Rushmore?

3. Charles Lindbergh completed his famous solo across the Atlantic Ocean in what year?

   1925   1927   1935   1939

4. Japan attacked Pearl Harbor on December 7 of what year?

   1935   1939   1941   1943

5. This famous Union general became president of the U.S. in 1869.

6. She became the first female Prime Minister of England.

7. Name the instrument used to measure the intensity of earthquakes.

8. This science is the study of all living things.

9. Abner Doubleday is given credit for developing this game.

10. Fenway Park is home to what team?

11. This form of poetry is named for a city in Ireland.

12. Mikhail Baryshnikov is associated with what art form?

TRIVIA

13. In what state will you find the Grand Canyon?

14. What state was the first to ratify the U.S. Constitution?

15. Where will you find Everglades National Park?

16. Alaska became a state in what year?

        1899   1959   1950   1962

17. This term is used to describe the water content of air.

18. Marie Curie was responsible for the discovery of this element.

19. He was a boy-king of ancient Egypt. The discovery of his tomb revealed many treasures.

20. Among many other things, he invented the victrola, the motion picture camera and the incandescent light bulb.

21. In what sport would you use the following terms:

        steal   pop-up   error   double-play

22. How many teams are in the National Football League?

23. This American artist is famous for painting a picture of his mother.

24. What U.S. poet is famous for creating the line of poetry, "....and miles to go before I sleep...."?

TRIVIA

1. What is the street address of the White House?

2. What state shares its name with one of the Great Lakes?

3. In what year was Sputnik launched?

   1955   1957   1962   1964

4. What city served as the first U.S. capital?

5. This common household item has NaCl as its chemical formula.

6. The science of rocks and minerals is _____.

7. This German scientist developed the thermometer and also a scale of temperature measurement that bears his name.

8. This famous American pilot was "lost at sea" during her Pacific flight in 1937.

9. John McEnroe is a champion in what sport?

10. What is the home of the N.B.A. Celtics?

11. This dance form is known as the national folk dance of Poland.

12. This 19th century author wrote many books, including <u>Oliver Twist</u> and <u>A Christmas Carol</u>.

TRIVIA

13. Name the children's story in which a spider saves a pig's life.

14. This cartoonist is responsible for giving us Lucy, Linus and Marcie.

15. Animals without backbones are called _____.

16. Airplanes must overcome this force to take-off.

17. You will find the Sphinx in what African country?

18. Which American state is really a group of islands?

19. These daring sailors "discovered" North America long before Columbus.

20. This ship carried the Pilgrims to Massachusetts from England.

21. This song is the national anthem of the United States of America.

22. Name the first American female crew member of a space shuttle flight.

23. Name the woman author best known for Little Women.

24. This popular game is called "football" in many countries; Americans call it by another name. What is it?

TRIVIA

1. In what American city will you find the "Golden Gate Bridge"?

2. What country is also a continent?

3. In what year did the U. S. Civil War begin?

   1861   1868   1870   1880

4. Water boils at ____° F. (At sea level)

5. _____ are the particles that travel around the center of an atom.

6. This famous Greek of the late sixth century B.C. is best known for his fables.

7. In what novel will you find the characters Becky, Tom, and Aunt Polly?

8. This U. S. President was responsible for making the Louisiana Purchase.

9. This man directed the movie Star Wars.

10. This composer is known as the "Waltz King."

11. This man was the first human to walk on the moon.

12. He holds the major league record for most home runs.

TRIVIA

13. Which explorer sailed "The Half Moon" during his voyage to America?

    Ponce DeLeon   Henry Hudson   Ferdinand Magellen

14. This famous French scientist proved that bacteria could spread disease.

15. In which nation would you find the Louvre Art Museum?

16. Located in Cambridge, Massachusetts, this famous college was founded in 1636.

17. The terms: trotters, pacers, and sulkies are associated with a popular sport. Name it!

18. What was the chief musical instrument of the ancient Greeks?

19. Whose face is pictured on the U. S. hundred dollar bill?

20. What is the name given to Egyptian picture writing?

21. In which part of the body would you find the retina, the cornea, and the iris?

22. Name the mountain range of south-central Asia that includes the highest peak in the world.

23. Who is the creator of the "Muppets"?

24. This famous Scottish writer authored A Child's Garden of Verses.

TRIVIA

1. Which American city is known as the "Windy City"?

2. In what sport would you use the following terms?

   fairway   apron   club   driver

3. What is the name given to scientists who study the weather?

4. Who authored The Tales of Peter Rabbit?

5. Which style of art did Picasso help to create?

   Impressionism   Surrealism   Cubism   Realism

6. In what year did a human first walk on the moon?

   1972   1969   1976   1963

7. What is the particle in the nucleus of an atom that has no charge?

8. Name the two football teams that met in the first Superbowl Game!

9. When the Owl and the Pussycat went to sea, what did they take along?

10. In which American national park will you find "Old Faithful"?

11. Name the two nations who opposed each other in the War of 1812?

12. Which of the following musical instruments does not belong to the woodwind group?

    clarinet   flute   oboe   trombone

TRIVIA

13. Which part of the body includes the humerus and the ulna?

14. In what country are the following cities located?

    Montreal   Quebec   Winnipeg   Toronto

15. Name the Italian trader whose travels to China gave Europeans their first information about the Far East.

16. How many sides does a pentagon have?

17. The name's the same: a U.S. President and a manufacturer and designer of cars.

18. In the nursery rhyme, "Baa, Baa, Black Sheep," how many bags of wool were full?

19. Which baseball team has won the most World Series competitions?

20. Name the highest elevation in the U.S.

21. In the book Treasure Island, Jim Hawkins meets a cunning pirate. Name him!

22. What is the term given to the condition of sleep in which some animals spend the winter?

23. This nineteenth century French artist is noted for his style of art called "pointillism."

24. He held the heavyweight boxing title longer than any other boxer (from 1937 to 1949). Name him!

TRIVIA

1. What is the name given to the imaginary line on a globe that runs from pole to pole and passes through Greenwich, England?

2. What sport do Tom Watson, Nancy Lopez, Arnold Palmer and Ben Crenshaw play?

3. Name the inert, colorless and odorless gas that is used in incandescent lightbulbs and radio tubes.

4. What are the minute blood vessels that connect the arteries and the veins in the human body?

5. Name the type of rocks that are natural magnets.

6. What is the title of the exciting book by Daniel Defoe that tells of the adventures of a man who is shipwrecked on an island?

7. This lovable bear was created by A. A. Milne as a companion for Christopher Robin.

8. Where would you find the Negev Desert?

    Egypt   Iraq   Israel   Kenya

9. Which state is known as "The Garden State"?

10. For what type of music is John Philip Sousa known?

11. The name's the same: The fifth president of the U.S. and the beautiful blonde star of the film, Gentlemen Prefer Blondes.

12. Where did George Washington and his troops spend the cold winter of 1777?

TRIVIA

13. He faced Stephen Douglas in a series of famous debates.

14. In what state will you find Pike's Peak?

15. The reaction in which an atomic nucleus splits into fragments is known as _____.

16. How many miles in a marathon race?

17. Samuel Clemens was the real name of what American author?

18. He experimented with and developed the laws of gravity.

19. On what continent will you find the Cape of Good Hope?

20. According to the fairy tale, what made Rapunzel famous?

21. The United States' purchase of Alaska from Russia was once known as _____'s folly. Name that American Secretary of State.

22. There was a rush of migrants to California in 1849 because of this.

23. She founded the American Red Cross.

24. How many separate events make up the decathlon?

ANSWERS

T-1

1. Philadelphia	13. Peoples' Republic of China
2. Georgia	14. Chess
3. 98.6°F	15. Robin Hood
4. Arthur	16. 3
5. Paul Revere	17. 8
6. Steven Spielberg	18. Wright Brothers
7. Metamorphosis	19. 14
8. Flouride	20. Texas
9. Baseball	21. Harp
10. Ice Hockey	22. Betsy Ross
11. Leonardo da Vinci	23. Basketball
12. Laura Ingalls Wilder	24. Lava (magma)

T-2

1. Washington, D.C.	13. Arizona
2. South Dakota	14. Delaware
3. 1927	15. Florida
4. 1941	16. 1959
5. Ulysses S. Grant	17. Humidity
6. Margaret Thatcher	18. Radium (or Polonium)
7. Seismometer (or Seismograph)	19. Tutankhamun (-amen)
8. Biology	20. Thomas Edison
9. Baseball	21. Baseball
10. Boston Red Sox	22. 28
11. Limerick	23. James Whistler
12. Ballet	24. Robert Frost

T-3

1. 1600 Pennsylvania Avenue	13. Charlotte's Web
2. Michigan	14. Charles Schulz
3. 1957	15. invertebrates
4. New York	16. Gravity
5. Salt	17. Egypt
6. Geology	18. Hawaii
7. Farenheit	19. Vikings
8. Amelia Earhart	20. Mayflower
9. Tennis	21. "Star Spangled Banner"
10. Boston	22. Sally Ride
11. Polka	23. Louisa May Alcott
12. Charles Dickens	24. Soccer

ANSWERS

T-4

1. San Francisco
2. Australia
3. 1861
4. 212
5. Electrons
6. Aesop
7. The Adventures of Tom Sawyer
8. Thomas Jefferson
9. George Lucas
10. Johann Strauss, the Younger
11. Neil Armstrong
12. Hank Aaron
13. Henry Hudson
14. Louis Pasteur
15. France
16. Harvard
17. Harness Racing
18. Lyre
19. Benjamin Franklin's
20. Hieroglyphics
21. Eye
22. Himalayas
23. Jim Henson
24. Robert Louis Stevenson

T-5

1. Chicago
2. Golf
3. Meteorologists
4. Beatrix Potter
5. Cubism
6. 1969
7. Neutron
8. Green Bay Packers & Kansas City Chiefs
9. Honey and Money
10. Yellowstone
11. America & Great Britain
12. Trombone
13. Arm
14. Canada
15. Marco Polo
16. 5
17. Ford
18. 3
19. New York Yankees
20. Mt. McKinley
21. Long John Silver
22. Hibernation
23. Seurat
24. Joe Lewis

T-6

1. Prime Meridian
2. Golf
3. Argon
4. Capillaries
5. Lodestones
6. Robinson Crusoe
7. Winnie The Pooh
8. Israel
9. New Jersey
10. Marches
11. Monroe
12. Valley Forge, PA
13. Abraham Lincoln
14. Colorado
15. Fission
16. 26
17. Mark Twain
18. Sir Isaac Newton
19. Africa
20. Long Hair
21. William Henry Seward
22. Gold
23. Clara Barton
24. 10

MATH AND LOGIC QUIZ

Suggested Time: 15 minutes

(2 minutes for directions)

(13 minutes for competitive activity)

In this section, competition is based on math computation, reasoning and problem solving skills. There are six different types of activities.

1. Missing Signs - Using the operational signs, students are asked to construct a true number sentence.

    Example: 2__5__3 = 13   2 x 5 + 3 = 13

2. Word Problems - Students must use their problem solving skills in order to complete problems of varying difficulty.

3. Computation Code - Using the hints provided, students must discover number-for-letter values.

    Example: A = __4__   A E

    E = __0__   + A E   Hint B = 8

                      B E

4. Patterns - Students supply the missing number that relates to the other numbers in the given number pattern.

    Example: 5, 7, 10, __14__   (+2 +3 +4)

5. Circle Math - Students must place numbers in the circles in order to correctly complete the problem. There may be more than one correct number arrangement for each problem.

    Example: Put a number in each circle so that the sum of each side is equal to the number in the center.

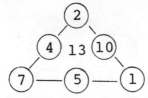

6. Math Trivia - Students must respond to a variety of math questions. They must circle or fill in the correct answer.

Scoring: One point is scored for each correct answer. In the MISSING SIGNS and PATTERNS activities, score one point for each correct A and B response. In scoring the COMPUTATION CODE activity, all values must be correct in order to score a point. In CIRCLE MATH, the entire problem must be correct in order to score a point. In MATH TRIVIA and WORD PROBLEMS some problems ask more than one question. The teacher may choose to award partial credit. Tally the total for each team and record it on the scoresheet next to the team name.

MATH AND LOGIC QUIZ

1. <u>Fill in the missing signs</u> to make the following number sentences true. Use +, -, x, or ÷.

   a. 14 3 6 2 = 33

   b. 14 3 6 2 = 5

2. <u>Solve the problem!</u> Write your answer in the space below.

   Elaine collected 5 dimes, 7 nickels, 5 quarters, a half dollar and 7 pennies. How much money did she have in all?

3. <u>Computation Code</u>: Name the value for B & C. (No 2 letters have the same value and none is greater than 9.)

   B =   C

   C =   C

                           + C
                           ─────
                           B C

4. <u>Supply the missing numerals</u> to complete the following patterns.

   a. 4, 2, 1, 1/2, 1/4, 1/8, _____ ?

   b. 10, 20, 40, 80, _____ ?

5. <u>Circle Math</u>: Put a number in each circle so that the sum of each side of the triangle is equal to the number in the center. Use the numbers 1 to 6 in this problem and use each number only once.

6. <u>Math Trivia</u>: What is the name given to a six sided figure? Circle the correct answer.

   pentagon   hexagon   octagon

MATH AND LOGIC QUIZ

1. <u>Fill in the missing signs</u> to make the number sentences true.
    Use +, -, x, or ÷.

    a. 3 3 9 = 1

    b. 4 3 2 = 6

2. <u>Solve the following problem</u>! Write your answer in the space
    below.

    Fred is on a camp-out and has thrown all of his socks into a
    bag. It is still dark when he gets dressed. He knows he has
    6 blue socks, 6 white socks and 6 grey socks. What is the
    greatest number of socks he'll have to pull out to be sure of
    getting a matching pair?

3. <u>Computation Code</u>: Name the values for A, B, and D. (No 2
    letters have the same value and none is greater than 9.)

    A =

    B =

    D =

       A B
     + B D
     ——————
       E C

    <u>HINT</u>
    E = 6
    C = 4

4. <u>Supply the missing numerals</u> in the following patterns:

    a. 1, 3, 6, _____

    b. 20, 15, 11, 8, _____

5. <u>Put a number in each circle</u> so that the sum of each side of
    the triangle is equal to the number in the center. Use each
    number only once.

    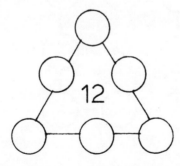

6. <u>Math Trivia</u>: In which math operation will you use a <u>subtrahend</u>?

MATH AND LOGIC QUIZ

1. <u>Fill in the missing signs</u> to make the following statements true. Use +, -, x, or ÷.

    a. 100   25   3   5 = 30

    b. 100   25   3   5 = 7

2. <u>Solve the problem</u>! Write your answer in the space below.

    If 4 times a certain number is increased by 3, the answer is five times the original number. What is that number?

3. Computation Code: Name the values for A and E. (No 2 letters have the same value and none is greater than 9.)

A =	A E	HINT
E =	+ A E	B = 8
	B E	

4. <u>Supply the missing numerals</u> to complete the following patterns.

    a.   2, 4, 6, 12, 14, _____?

    b.   2, 6, 9, 11, 12, _____?

5. <u>Circle Math</u>: Put a number in each circle so that the sum of each side of the square is equal to the number in the center. Use the numbers 1, 2, 3, 4, 5, 6, 8, and 9. Use each number only once.

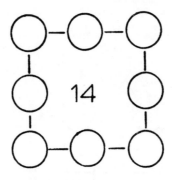

6. <u>Math Trivia</u>: How many quarts are in 13 gallons?

MATH AND LOGIC QUIZ

1. <u>Fill in the missing signs</u> to make the following number sentences true. Use +, -, x, or ÷.

    a. 12 2 6 10 = 28
    b. 12 2 6 10 = 70

2. <u>Solve the problem!</u> Write your answers in the spaces below.

    Four boys decided to combine their 35 marbles. Scott had twice as many as Andrew. Steve had three times as many as Peter. Andrew had 1/7 of the marbles. How many marbles did each boy have?

    Scott _____   Steve _____   Peter _____   Andrew _____

3. <u>Computation Code</u>: Name the values for A and B. (No 2 letters have the same value and none is greater than 9.)

    A =   A B   HINT
                         + C A   D = 7
    B =   ─────   C = 1
                           B D

4. <u>Supply the missing numeral</u> to complete the following patterns.

    a. 2, 6, 5, 9, 8, _____?
    b. 3, 6, 10, 15, 21, _____?

5. <u>Circle Math</u>: Put a number in each circle so that the sum of each side of the triangle is equal to the number in the center. Use numbers 1 to 9 in this problem and use each number only once.

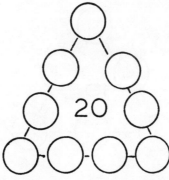

6. <u>Math Trivia</u>: Circle the name that is used to describe the distance around a circle.

    diameter   radius   circumference

MATH AND LOGIC QUIZ

1. <u>Fill in the missing signs</u> to make these number sentences
    true. Use +, -, x, or ÷.

    a. 5   5   4   10 = 10

    b. 2   4   2   4   = 4

2. <u>Solve the following problem!</u> Write your answer in the space
    below.

    A farmer collects 100 eggs from the henhouse. Ten percent
    of the eggs have cracks, another 10% are otherwise defective.
    How many eggs are left to take to the market?

3. <u>Computation Code:</u> Name the values for C and D. (No 2 letters
    have the same value and none is greater than 9.)

	A C	HINT
C =	+ C D	E = 4
D =	E A	A = 3

4. <u>Supply the missing numerals</u> in the following patterns.

    a. 3, 9, 27, 81, _____?

    b. 3, 6, 18, 72, _____?

5. <u>Circle Math:</u> Put a number in each circle so that the sum of
    each side of the triangle is equal to the number in the cen-
    ter. Use the numbers 1, 3, 4, 6, 8, and 10. Use each number
    only once.

6. <u>Math Trivia:</u> Circle the aspect of math that involves the
    study of cubes, triangles, cylinders, etc.

    tangrams   geometry   logarithms   algebra

MATH AND LOGIC QUIZ

1. **Fill in the missing signs** to make these number sentences true. Use +, -, x, or ÷.

    a. 5 3 5 4 = 5

    b. 6 4 3 6 = 5

2. **Solve the following problem!** Write your answer in the space below.

    Two men agree to paint a house for $1000.00. One man works for eight days, the other works for twelve days. How much should the first man be paid for eight days' work?

3. **Computation Code:** Name the values for P, Q, R, T, and Z. (No 2 letters have the same value and none is greater than 9.)

P =	T =	X Y Z	HINT
Q =	Z =	+ P Q Y	S = 1
R =		S R R T	X = 5
			Y = 7

4. **Supply the missing numerals** in the following patterns.

    a. 15, 27, 39, 51, _____?

    b. 8, 12, 6, 10, 4, _____?

5. **Circle Math:** Put a number in each circle so that the sum of each side of the triangle is equal to the number in the center. Use only the numbers 1, 2, 4, 5, 7, and 10. Use each number only once.

    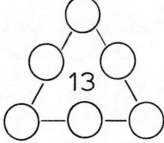

6. **Math Trivia:** Circle the correct answer for the number of degrees in a circle.

    80°   90°   180°   360°

MATH AND LOGIC QUIZ

1. Fill in the missing signs to make the following number statements true. Use +, -, x, or ÷.

    a. 16   2   7   5   3 = 13

    b. 16   2   7   5   3 = 30

2. Solve the problem! Write your answer in the space below.

    Mr. Hamilton received six coins. One half of the coins are nickels. The nickels make up one fourth of the total money value. What coins does Mr. Hamilton have?

3. Computation Code: Name the values for A, C, D and T. (No 2 letters have the same value and none is greater than 9.)

    A =

    C =   C A T   HINT
                                G = 8
    D =   + R A T   O = 6
                 -------   R = 7
                 D O G
    T =

4. Supply the missing numerals to complete the following patterns.

    a.   4, 7, 6, 9, 8, _____?

    B.   7, 10, 30, 33, 99, _____?

5. Circle Math: Put a number in each circle so that the sum of each side of the square is equal to the number in the center. Use the numbers 1, 2, 3, 5, 6, 7, 8 and 9. Use each number only once.

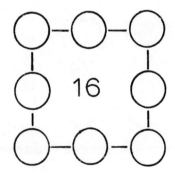

6. Math Trivia: What is the name that is a unit of speed equal to a nautical mile per hour?

MATH AND LOGIC QUIZ

1. <u>Fill in the missing signs</u> to make these number sentences true. Use +, -, x, or ÷.

    a. 20   5   4 = 16

    b. 20   5   4   3 = 15

2. <u>Solve the following problem!</u> Write your answer in the space below.

    Four boys were outside Mr. Smith's house when one of them threw the ball through the window. Mr. Smith knew that three of the boys always told the truth and one of them always lied. After listening to their statements, Mr. Smith knew who did it. Do you?

    > Bob: "Jason threw the ball."
    > Tom: "I didn't throw the ball."
    > Jason: "Neil did it."
    > Neil: "Jason lied when he said I did it."

3. <u>Computation Code</u>: Name the values of A and E. (No 2 letters have the same value and none is greater than 9.)

    A =   A J   <u>HINT</u>

    E =   x E   J = 5

                 D J   D = 4

4. <u>Supply the missing numerals</u> in the following patterns:

    a. 3, 6, 4, 8, 6, _____?

    b. 2, 6, 3, 9, 6, _____?

5. <u>Circle Math</u>: Put a number in each circle so that the sum of each side of the triangle is equal to the number in the center. Use the numbers 3, 5, 6, 7, 8, and 9. Use each number only once.

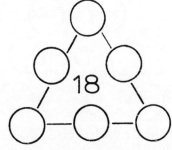

6. <u>Math Trivia</u>: What do we call a number which can only be divided evenly by itself and one?

MATH AND LOGIC QUIZ

1. **Fill in the missing signs** to make the following number sentences true. Use +, -, x, or ÷.

    a. 2   4   10   3   8 = 14
    b. 2   4   10   3   8 = 28

2. **Solve the problem!** Write your answer in the space below.

    There were six more players on the Wildcats than there were on the Orioles. Five players changed from the Wildcats to the Orioles, so that now there are twice as many players on the Orioles than on the Wildcats. How many players were on the Wildcats' team before the change?

3. **Computation Code:** Name the values for F, M, O and W. (No 2 letters have the same value and none is greater than 9.)

    F =

    O =

    W =

    ```
      S U M
    + F U N
      N O W
    ```

    HINT
    M = 2
    N = 7
    S = 6
    U = 4

4. **Supply the missing numerals** to complete the following patterns.

    a.   3, 11, 18, 24, 29, _____?
    b.   4, 5, 6, 8, 10, 13, _____?

5. **Circle Math:** Put a number in each circle so that the sum of each side of the triangle is equal to the number in the center. Use numbers 1 to 9 in this problem and use each number only once.

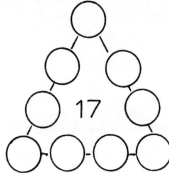

6. **Math Trivia:** What numbers do the following Roman numerals represent?

    XL = _____   CM = _____   MDCXLV = _____

MATH AND LOGIC QUIZ

1. <u>Fill in the missing signs</u> to make these number sentences true. Use +, -, x, or ÷.

   a.   20   5   10   3 = 7
   b.   30   6   6   3 = 10

2. <u>Solve the following problem!</u> Write your answer in the space below.

   At 45 mph a car travels 1½ miles. How long does it take the car to cover that distance?

3. <u>Computation Code</u>: Name the values for D and J. (No 2 letters have the same value and none is greater than 9.)

   D =   A J   <u>HINT</u>
                   - D E   A = 7
   J =   ─────   E = 2
                     E A

4. <u>Supply the missing numerals</u> to complete the following patterns.

   a.   7, 10, 14, 19, 25, _____?
   b.   9, 16, 11, 18, 13, _____?

5. <u>Circle Math</u>: Put a number in each circle so that the sum of each side of the triangle is equal to the number in the center of the triangle. Use the numbers 1, 2, 3, 5, 6, and 7. Use each number only once.

14

6. <u>Math Trivia</u>: This has been used as a type of manual calculator in the Orient for centuries. What is it?

73

MATH AND LOGIC QUIZ

1. <u>Fill in the missing signs</u> to make these number sentences true. Use +, -, x, or ÷.

      a. 6 6 3 2 = 24

      b. 24 2 6 3 = 6

2. <u>Solve the following problem!</u> Write your answer in the space below.

In the township soccer league there are 300 players. Boys outnumber girls 5 to 1. How many girls are members of the soccer league?

3. <u>Computation Code:</u> Find the values for A, D, E, and G. (No 2 letters have the same value and none is greater than 9.)

A =

D =

E =

G =

```
  A B C
+ D E C
-------
  C G G
```

HINT

B = 7

C = 5

4. <u>Supply the missing numerals</u> in the following patterns.

    a. 12, 9, 14, 11, 16, _____?

    b. 4, 12, 9, 27, 24, _____?

5. <u>Circle Math:</u> Put a number in each circle so that the sum of each side of the triangle is equal to the number in the center of the triangle. Use the numbers 2, 3, 4, 5, 7, and 9. Use each number only once.

6. <u>Math Trivia:</u> What does the symbol $\sqrt{}$ represent?

74

MATH AND LOGIC QUIZ

1. Fill in the missing signs to make the following number sentences
    true. Use +, -, x, or ÷.

           a. 8 4 7 5 12 = 7

           b. 8 4 7 5 12 = 17

2. Solve the problem! Write your answers in the spaces below.

    Ed is two years older than Ron. Their father is twice Ed's age.
    The three ages total 78. Find their ages.

         Ed _____   Ron _____   Father _____

3. Computation Code: Name the values for C, D, P, and T. (No 2
    letters have the same value and none is greater than 9.)

    C =
    D =   C A N   HINT
               + P A T   A = 4
    P =   A D D   N = 6
    T =

4. Supply the missing numerals to complete the following patterns.

           a. 20, 17, 18, 15, 16, _____?

           b. 1, 3, 7, 13, 21, _____?

5. Circle Math: Put a number in each circle so that the sum of
    each side of the square is equal to the number in the center.
    Use the numbers 1, 2, 4, 5, 6, 7, 8, and 9.
    Use each number only once.

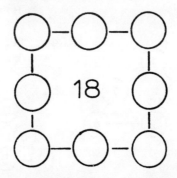

6. Math Trivia: What is the branch of mathematics in which symbols,
    usually letters of the alphabet, represent numbers?

ANSWERS

ML-1

1. a. 14 - 3 x 6 ÷ 2 = 33
   b. 14 x 3 ÷ 6 - 2 = 5

2. $2.67

3. B = 1
   C = 5

4. a. $\frac{1}{16}$
   b. 160

5.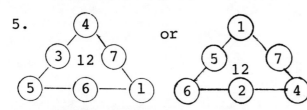

6. Hexagon

ML-2

1. a. 3 x 3 ÷ 9 = 1
   b. 4 x 3 ÷ 2 = 6

2. 4

3. A = 5
   B = 1
   D = 3

4. a. 10 (+2+3+4)
   b. 6 (-5-4-3-2)

5.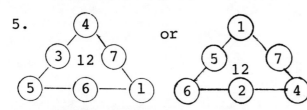

6. Subtraction

ML-3

1. a. 100 - 25 ÷ 3 + 5 = 30
   b. 100 ÷ 25 x 3 - 5 = 7

2. 3

3. A = 4
   E = 0

4. a. 28 (x2+2)
   b. 12 (+4+3+2+1+0)

5.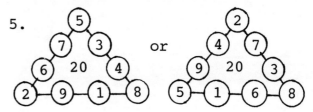

6. 52 quarts

ML-4

1. a. 12 x 2 - 6 + 10 = 28
   b. 12 - 2 x 6 + 10 = 70

2. Scott = 10
   Steve = 15
   Peter = 5
   Andrew = 5

3. A = 3
   B = 4

4. a. 12 (+4-1)
   b. 28 (+3+4+5+6+7)

5.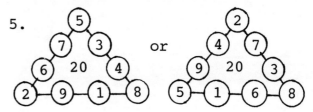

6. Circumference

ANSWERS

ML-5

1. a. $5 \times 5 \times 4 \div 10 = 10$
   b. $2 \times 4 \times 2 \div 4 = 4$

2. 80 eggs

3. C = 1
   D = 2

4. a. 243 (x3)
   b. 360 (x2x3x4x5)

5.

6. Geometry

ML-6

1. a. $5 \times 3 + 5 \div 4 = 5$
   b. $6 + 4 \times 3 \div 6 = 5$

2. $400

3. P = 4   P = 4
   Q = 3   Q = 2
   R = 0   or   R = 0
   T = 9   T = 6
   Z = 2   Z = 9

4. a. 63 (+12)
   b. 8 (+4-6)

5.

6. 360°

ML-7

1. a. $16 - 2 \div 7 \times 5 + 3 = 13$
   b. $16 \div 2 + 7 - 5 \times 3 = 30$

2. 3 nickels, 2 dimes, & 1 quarter

3. A = 3
   C = 2
   D = 9
   T = 4

4. a. 11 (+3-1)
   b. 102 (+3x3)

5.

6. Knot

ML-8

1. a. $20 \div 5 \times 4 = 16$
   b. $25 - 5 \div 4 \times 3 = 15$

*2. Jason (See note below)

3. A = 1
   E = 3

4. a. 12 (x2-2)
   b. 18 (x3-3)

5.

6. Prime number

* If Jason had been telling the truth,
Neil and Bob would have been lying.
Since only 1 boy could have lied,
Jason must not have been telling the
truth.

ANSWERS

ML-9

1. a. 2 x 4 + 10 ÷ 3 + 8 = 14
   b. 2 + 4 x 10 ÷ 3 + 8 = 28

2. 9 players

3. F = 1
   O = 8
   W = 9

4. a. 33 (+8+7+6+5+4)
   b. 16 (+1+1+2+2+3+3)

5.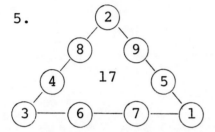

6. XL = 40, CM = 900, and
   MDCXLV = 1,645

ML-10

1. a. 20 x 5 ÷ 10 - 3 = 7
   b. 30 ÷ 6 x 6 ÷ 3 = 10

2. 2 minutes

3. D = 5
   J = 9

4. a. 32 (+3+4+5+6+7)
   b. 20 (+7-5)

5.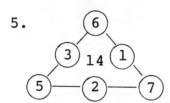

6. Abacus

ML-11

1. a. 6 x 6 ÷ 3 x 2 = 24
   b. 24 ÷ 2 ÷ 6 x 3 = 6

2. 50 girls

3. A = 1   A = 3
   D = 3   D = 1
   E = 2   or   E = 2
   G = 0   G = 0

4. a. 13 (-3+5)
   b. 72 (x3-3)

5.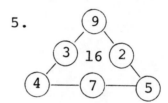

6. Square root

ML-12

1. a. 8 ÷ 4 x 7 + 5 - 12 = 7
   b. 8 x 4 - 7 ÷ 5 + 12 = 17

2. Ed = 20
   Ron = 18
   Father = 40

3. C = 3   C = 1
   D = 8   D = 8
   P = 1   or   P = 3
   T = 2   T = 2

4. a. 13 (-3+1)
   b. 31 (+2+4+6+8)

5.

6. Algebra

78

LANGUAGE PUZZLERS

Suggested Time: 15 minutes

(2 minutes for directions)

(13 minutes for competitive activity)

The activities in this section test a variety of language skills. Each page contains seven different puzzlers.

1. Double Definitions - Students are asked to supply a single word that fits each set of two definitions.

   Ex. part of eye / flowering plant = iris

2. Word Riddles - Students are challenged to discover compounds and other words by combining two definitions.

   Ex. something to read / something in which to carry things = bookbag

3. Anagrams - Students are asked to rearrange letters of words or phrases to form new ones.

   Ex. NOW = OWN

4. Word Chains - By changing only one letter in each link, students must form complete words from start to finish.

   Ex. LIKE - BIKE - BAKE - CAKE

5. Analogies - Students are asked to find the relationship between the first two words in order to complete the analogies.

   Ex. car : garage :: horse : stable

6. Misspelled Words - Students are asked to circle the one misspelled word in each group of words.

7. Word Cubes - Using the clues provided, students are to give the correct rhyming words. The center word provides a clue to the rhyming pattern.

   Scoring: One point is scored for each correct answer. Give credit for each part of the WORD CHAIN and WORD CUBE. If the activity is conducted as a team effort, score one point for each correct team answer. Tally each team's total and record it on the scoresheet next to the team name.

LANGUAGE PUZZLERS

1. <u>Double Definitions</u>: Supply a single word that fits each set of two definitions.

    a. a letter of the alphabet / used in playing golf _____

    b. a large mass of stone / to move back and forth _____

    c. part of your mouth / a sticky, chewy substance _____

    d. where the road divides / implement used for eating _____

2. <u>Word Riddle</u>: What word do you get when you combine a dwelling with a means of transportation?

3. <u>Anagrams</u>: Rearrange the letters in these words to form new words. Example: TEA = EAT

    a. CARE = _____   b. WEST = _____

4. <u>Word Chain</u>: By changing only one letter at a time, fill in each link with a new word to form the last word given. Example: LIKE - BIKE - BAKE - CAKE

    PUNT ( ) ( ) PASS

5. <u>Analogies</u>: Complete each analogy so that the second half of the set relates in the same way as the first half. Example: car : garage :: horse : stable

    a. lead : pencil :: film : _____?

    b. penny : money :: corn : _____?

6. <u>Misspelled Words</u>: Circle the misspelled word in the following group.

    untill   division   vacation   career

7. <u>Word Cube</u>: Using the clues provided, fill in the spaces in the cube with the correct rhyming words. They must rhyme with the word in the center of the cube.

    1. a story
    2. a strong wind
    3. an instrument used
       for weighing
    4. a sea mammal

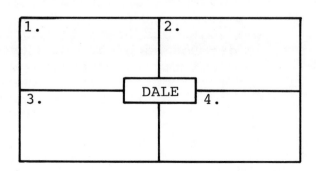

LANGUAGE PUZZLERS

1. <u>Double Definitions</u>: Supply a single word that fits each set of two definitions.

    a. a river bottom / furniture for sleeping _____

    b. a finger part / wood fastener _____

    c. a plant part / word basic _____

    d. a child's toy / highest part _____

2. <u>Word Riddle</u>: What romantic word do you get when you combine a substance that bees make with a part of the solar system?

3. <u>Anagrams</u>: Rearrange the letters in these words to form new words. Example: TEA = EAT

    a. NEWS = _____   b. THERE = _____

4. <u>Word Chain</u>: By changing only one letter at a time, fill in each link with a new word to form the last word given.
    Example: LIKE - BIKE - BAKE - CAKE

    TEA — __ — __ — MET

5. <u>Analogies</u>: Complete each analogy so that the second half of the set relates in the same way as the first half. Example: car : garage :: horse : stable

    a. nostril : face :: elbow : _____ ?

    b. snake : scales :: dog : _____ ?

6. <u>Misspelled Word</u>: Circle the misspelled word in the following group.

    mathamatics   allergy   syrup   ocelot

7. <u>Word Cube</u>: Using the clues provided, fill in the spaces in the cube with the correct rhyming words. They must rhyme with the word in the center of the cube.

    1.   a chicken
    2.   after nine
    3.   bear's home
    4.   not now

1.	2.
WHEN	
3.	4.

LANGUAGE PUZZLERS

1. Double Definitions: Supply a single word that fits each set of two definitions.

   a. part of the foot / kind of fish _____

   b. metallic element / instrument used to smooth cloth _____

   c. inner part of your hand / branchless, tropical tree _____

   d. a nocturnal mammal / sports equipment _____

2. Word Riddle: What word do you get when you combine a means of transportation with an animal that is kept home?

3. Anagram: Rearrange the letters in these words to form new words. Example: TEA = EAT

   a. SALT = _____   b. SKIN = _____

4. Word Chain: By changing only one letter at a time, fill in each link with a new word to form the last word given.
   Example: LIKE - BIKE - BAKE - CAKE

   HEAT (   ) (   ) (   ) COAT

5. Analogies: Complete each analogy so that the second half of the set relates in the same way as the first half. Example: car : garage :: horse : stable

   a. simple : difficult :: polite : _____?

   b. Bell : telephone :: Gutenberg : _____?

6. Misspelled Word: Circle the misspelled word in the following group.

   volunteer   immediate   bandage   survay

7. Word Cube: Using the clues provided, fill in the spaces in the cube with the correct rhyming words. They must rhyme with the word in the center of the cube.

   1.   imitate cruelly
   2.   group of animals
   3.   a baby's toy
   4.   a sudden, painful experience

1.	2.
3. SOCK	4.

LANGUAGE PUZZLERS

1. Double Definitions: Supply a single word that fits each set of two definitions.

   a. in good health / a source of water _____

   b. a chocolate dessert / a junior Girl Scout _____

   c. a bouyant rescue device/ a candy _____

   d. to hurry / a grasslike plant _____

2. Word Riddle: What word do you get when you combine a part of the body and an Edison invention?

3. Anagrams: Rearrange the letters in these words to form new words. Example: TEA = EAT

   a. STARE = _____   b. BEAR = _____

4. Word Chain: By changing only one letter at a time, fill in each link with a new word to form the last word given. Example: LIKE - BIKE - BAKE - CAKE

   BEAT ────── ────── FEEL

5. Analogies: Complete each analogy so that the second half of the set relates in the same way as the first half. Example: car : garage :: horse: stable

      a. equatorial : hot :: polar : _____?

      b. kitten : cat :: foal : _____?

6. Misspelled Word: Circle the misspelled word in the following group.

       poinsetta   gardenia   pansy   azalea

7. Word Cube: Using the clues provided, fill in the spaces in the cube with the correct rhyming words. They must rhyme with the word in the center of the cube.

   1. a tree type
   2. to eat
   3. okay
   4. 3 x 3

1.	2.
LINE
3.	4.

83

LANGUAGE PUZZLERS

1. Double Definitions: Supply a single word that fits each set of two definitions.

    a. sore on your foot / something oversentimental _____

    b. cowardly / lemon colored _____

    c. for deposits / river's edge _____

    d. a season / a coil _____

2. Word Riddle: What word do you get when you combine a long strip of wood and movement on foot?

3. Anagrams: Rearrange the letters in these words to form new words. Example: TEA = EAT

    a. Trish = _____   b. Tips = _____

4. Word Chain: By changing only one letter at a time, fill in each link with a new word to form the last word given. Example: LIKE - BIKE - BAKE - CAKE

    SEA) (MET) (MAN

5. Analogies: Complete each analogy so that the second half of the set relates in the same way as the first half. Example: car : garage :: horse : stable

    a. mango : fruit :: toucan : _____ ?

    b. monarch : butterfly :: cobra : _____ ?

6. Misspelled Word: Circle the misspelled word in the following group.

    erasable   delicious   baloon   chocolate

7. Word Cube: Using the clues provided, fill in the spaces in the cube with the correct rhyming words. They must rhyme with the word in the center of the cube.

    1. a window part
    2. a small path
    3. on a horse or lion
    4. walking aid

1.	2.
SANE	
3.	4.

LANGUAGE PUZZLERS

1. **Double Definitions:** Supply a single word that fits each set of two definitions.

   a. to abandon / an arid, sandy area _____
   b. an outdoor area near a building / a measure of length _____
   c. a percussion instrument / part of the ear _____
   d. a division of a building / a tale _____

2. **Word Riddle:** What word do you get when you combine a large male mammal and an instrument used for writing?

3. **Anagrams:** Rearrange the letters in these words to form new words. Example: TEA = EAT

   a. LISTEN = _____   b. TEACH = _____

4. **Word Chain:** By changing only one letter at a time, fill in each link with a new word to form the last word given. Example: LIKE - BIKE - BAKE - CAKE

   READ ⬭ ⬭ ⬭ ⬭ BOOK

5. **Analogies:** Complete each analogy so that the second half of the set relates in the same way as the first half. Example: car : garage :: horse : stable

   a. Albany : New York :: Atlanta: _____?
   b. sandal : foot :: fedora : _____?

6. **Misspelled Word:** Circle the misspelled word in the following group.

   mobile   bulletin   disipline   exist

7. **Word Cube:** Using the clues provided, fill in the spaces in the cube with the correct rhyming words. They must rhyme with the word in the center of the cube.

   1. part of a car
   2. gentle, sensitive
   3. an appliance used for mixing
   4. one who pays

1.	2.
GENDER	
3.	4.

85

LANGUAGE PUZZLERS

1. <u>Double Definitions</u>: Supply a single word that fits each set of two definitions.

    a. tall tale / a sweater material _____

    b. animal home / writing implement _____

    c. uncooked bread / money _____

    d. unmarried girl / off target _____

2. <u>Word Riddle</u>: What word do you get when you combine a division of time and a drinking vessel?

3. <u>Anagrams</u>: Rearrange the letters in these words to form new words. Example: TEA = EAT

    a. HORSE = _____   b. NOTES = _____

4. <u>Word Chain</u>: By changing only one letter at a time, fill in each link with a new word to form the last word given. Example: LIKE - BIKE - BAKE - CAKE

    ROLE ( ) ( ) ( ) PART

5. <u>Analogies</u>: Complete each analogy so that the second half of the set relates in the same way as the first half. Example: car : garage :: horse : stable

    a. knit : needle :: crochet : _____ ?

    b. tadpole : frog :: chrysalis : _____ ?

6. <u>Misspelled Word</u>: Circle the misspelled word in the following group.

    aligator   infectious   conscience   macaroon

7. <u>Word Cube</u>: Using the clues provided, fill in the spaces in the cube with the correct rhyming words. They must rhyme with the word in the center of the cube.

    1. small nail
    2. narrow opening
    3. in need of something
    4. raceway

1.	2.
3. BLACK	4.

LANGUAGE PUZZLERS

1. <u>Double Definitions</u>: Supply a single word that fits each set of two definitions.

    a. a large mammal / to endure _____

    b. tooth bed / type of tree _____

    c. a flavor / coin factory _____

    d. to make a line or dent / boy's name _____

2. <u>Word Riddle</u>: What word do you get when you combine having little length with a part of the body?

3. <u>Anagrams</u>: Rearrange the letters in these words to form new words. Example: TEA = EAT

    a. PANEL = _____   b. SLIME = _____

4. <u>Word Chain</u>: By changing only one letter at a time, fill in each link with a new word to form the last word given. Example: LIKE - BIKE - BAKE - CAKE

    LOVE ( ) ( ) ( ) HATE

5. <u>Analogies</u>: Complete each analogy so that the second half of the set relates in the same way as the first half. Example: car : garage :: horse : stable

    a. silk : fabric :: moss : _____?

    b. Sahara : desert :: Nile : _____?

6. <u>Misspelled Word</u>: Circle the misspelled word in the following group.

    beige   arogant   deceive   pentameter

7. <u>Word Cube</u>: Using the clues provided, fill in the spaces in the cube with the correct rhyming words. They must rhyme with the word in the center of the cube.

    1. an object
    2. with pong, a game
    3. jewelry
    4. a season

1.	2.
3. BRING	4.

LANGUAGE PUZZLERS

1. <u>Double Definitions</u>: Supply a single word that fits each set
of two definitions.

   a. to rip open / a drop of liquid from the eye _____

   b. to sell / bird of prey _____

   c. main tree part / large suitcase _____

   d. celebrities / constellation _____

2. <u>Word Riddle</u>: What word do you get when you combine a part of
the body with bad weather?

3. <u>Anagrams</u>: Rearrange the letters in these words to form new
words. Example: TEA = EAT

   a. CLAIMER = _____   b. MOAT = _____

4. <u>Word Chain</u>: By changing only one letter at a time, fill in
each link with a new word to form the last word given. Example: LIKE - BIKE - BAKE - CAKE

   TOAD ( ) ( ) ( ) BEAR

5. <u>Analogies</u>: Complete each analogy so that the second half of
the set relates in the same way as the first half. Example:
car : garage :: horse : stable

   a. geology : rocks :: paleontology : _____?

   b. hemotology : blood :: cardiology : _____?

6. <u>Misspelled Word</u>: Circle the misspelled word in the following
group.

   parallel   masquerade   immitation   casserole

7. <u>Word Cube</u>: Using the clues provided, fill in the spaces in the
cube with the correct rhyming words. They must rhyme with the
word in the center of the cube.

   1. a liquid cosmetic
   2. a disturbance
   3. a special affection
   4. an impression or feeling

1.	2.
MOTION	
3.	4.

LANGUAGE PUZZLERS

1. <u>Double Definitions</u>: Supply a single word that fits each set of two definitions.

   a. volleyball play / a heavy nail _____

   b. wondrous sights / eyeglasses _____

   c. intertwine / decorative fabric _____

   d. a color / part of a golf course _____

2. <u>Word Riddle</u>: What word do you get when you combine a deep hole in the ground with the act of dropping oneself?

3. <u>Anagrams</u>: Rearrange the letters in these words to form new words. Example: TEA = EAT

   a. FLIER = _____   b. EPARCH = _____

4. <u>Word Chain</u>: By changing only one letter at a time, fill in each link with a new word to form the last word given. Example: LIKE - BIKE - BAKE - CAKE

   PLATE ( ) ( ) ( ) SCANT

5. <u>Analogies</u>: Complete each analogy so that the second half of the set relates in the same way as the first half. Example: car : garage :: horse : stable

   a. carat : gem :: caliber : _____ ?

   b. "1,000 Lakes " : Minnesota :: "Land of Lincoln" : _____ ?

6. <u>Misspelled Word</u>: Circle the misspelled word in the following group.

   Albuquerque   abreviate   artichoke   minuend

7. <u>Word Cube</u>: Using the clues provided, fill in the spaces in the cube with the correct rhyming words. They must rhyme with the word in the center of the cube.

   1.   conceal
   2.   ocean change
   3.   margin, edge, or border
   4.   broad

1.	2.
3. RIDE	4.

LANGUAGE PUZZLERS

1. <u>Double Definition</u>: Supply a single word that fits each set of two definitions.

    a. high ranking scout / national bird _____

    b. appointment / type of palm tree _____

    c. a hint / the very end _____

    d. a gem / baseball field _____

2. <u>Word Riddle</u>: What word do you get when you combine a good friend and a playing card?

3. <u>Anagrams</u>: Rearrange the letters in these words to form new words. Example: TEA = EAT

    a. TABLE = _____   b. GLARE = _____

4. <u>Word Chain</u>: By changing only one letter at a time, fill in each link with a new word to form the last word given. Example: LIKE - BIKE - BAKE - CAKE

    SWIM   (____) (____) (____)   STOP

5. <u>Analogies</u>: Complete each analogy so that the second half of the set relates in the same way as the first half. Example: car : garage :: horse : stable

    a. lead : heavy :: aluminum : _____ ?

    b. egg roll : Chinese :: taco : _____ ?

6. <u>Misspelled Word</u>: Circle the misspelled word in the following group.

    surgeon   manganese   equate   chandeleir

7. <u>Word Cube</u>: Using the clues provided, fill in the spaces in the cube with the correct rhyming words. They must rhyme with the word in the center of the cube.

    1.   garden tool
    2.   sadness
    3.   enemy
    4.   fish eggs
    5.   foot part

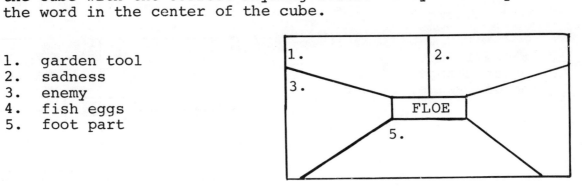

LANGUAGE PUZZLERS

1. <u>Double Definitions</u>: Supply a single word that fits each set of two definitions.

   a. disorder / armed forces eat here _____

   b. a heavy stick / an association of people _____

   c. a preserve / a crowd of people _____

   d. a device for rotary motion / a grouchy person _____

2. <u>Word Riddle</u>: What word do you get when you combine a division of time and something you do at night?

3. <u>Anagrams</u>: Rearrange the letters in these words to form new words. Example: TEA = EAT

   a. ELUDED = _____   b. ABRIDGE = _____

4. <u>Word Chain</u>: By changing only one letter at a time, fill in each link with a new word to form the last word given. Example: LIKE - BIKE - BAKE - CAKE

RAGE — ____ — PACT — ____ — ____ — FIST

5. <u>Analogies</u>: Complete each analogy so that the second half of the set relates in the same way as the first half. Example: car : garage :: horse : stable

   a. Renoir : Impressionism :: Dali : _____ ?

   b. puny : weak :: casual : _____ ?

6. <u>Misspelled Word</u>: Circle the misspelled word in the following group.

   consume   transparant   potential   exhort

7. <u>Word Cube</u>: Using the clues provided, fill in the spaces in the cube with the correct rhyming words. They must rhyme with the word in the center of the cube.

   1. precipitation
   2. to cringe in fear
   3. an endowment
   4. to authorize
   5. tall part of building

ANSWERS

(ANSWERS MAY VARY)

LP-1

1. a. tree   b. rock
   c. gum   d. fork
2. houseboat
3. a. acre or race
   b. stew
4. punt-pant-past-pass

5. a. camera
   b. vegetable or food
6. untill (until)
7. 1. tale   2. gale
   3. scale   4. whale

LP-2

1. a. bed   b. nail
   c. root   d. top
2. honeymoon
3. a. sewn
   b. three or ether
4. tea-ten-men-met; tea-sea-set-met;
   or tea-pea-pet-met

5. a. arm
   b. fur or hair
6. mathamatics (mathematics)
7. 1. hen   2. ten
   3. den   4. then

LP-3

1. a. sole   b. iron
   c. palm   d. bat
2. carpet
3. a. last
   b. sink
4. heat-beat-boat-coat or
   heat-meat-moat-coat

5. a. rude
   b. printing press (movable type)
6. survay (survey)
7. 1. mock   2. flock
   3. block   4. shock

LP-4

1. a. well   b. brownie
   c. lifesaver   d. rush
2. headlight
3. a. tears or tares
   b. bare
4. beat-feat-feet-feel or
   beat-beet-feet-feel

5. a. cold
   b. horse
6. poinsetta (poinsettia)
7. 1. pine   2. dine
   3. fine   4. nine

LP-5

1. a. corn   b. yellow
   c. bank   d. spring
2. boardwalk
3. a. shirt
   b. pits or spit
4. sea-set-met-men-man or
   sea-set-met-mat-man

5. a. bird
   b. snake
6. baloon (balloon)
7. 1. pane   2. lane
   3. mane   4. cane

LP-6

1. a. desert   b. yard
   c. drum   d. story
2. bullpen
3. a. silent, tinsel or enlist
   b. cheat
4. read-bead-beat-boat-boot-book

5. a. Georgia
   b. head
6. disipline (discipline)
7. 1. fender   2. tender
   3. blender   4. spender

LANGUAGE PUZZLERS

ANSWERS

LP-7

1. a. yarn b. pen
   c. dough d. miss
2. hourglass
3. a. shore
   b. stone
4. role-pole-pale-pare-part

5. a. hook
   b. butterfly, moth
6. aligator (alligator)
7. 1. tack 2. crack
   3. lack 4. track

LP-8

1. a. bear b. gum
   c. mint d. mark
2. shorthand
3. a. plane
   b. smile, limes or miles
4. love-dove-dote-date-hate or
   love-wove-wave-have-hate

5. a. plant
   b. river
6. arogant (arrogant)
7. 1. thing 2. ping
   3. ring 4. spring

LP-9

1. a. tear b. hawk
   c. trunk d. stars
2. brainstorm
3. a. miracle or reclaim
   b. atom
4. toad-load-lead-bead-bear

5. a. fossils
   b. heart
6. immitation (imitation)
7. 1. lotion 2. commotion
   3. devotion 4. notion

LP-10

1. a. spike b. spectacles
   b. lace d. green
2. pitfall
3. a. rifle
   b. preach
4. plate-plane-plant-slant-scant

5. a. gun or bullet
   b. Illinois
6. abreviate (abbreviate)
7. 1. hide 2. tide
   3. side 4. wide

LP-11

1. a. eagle b. date
   c. tip d. diamond
2. palace
3. a. bleat
   b. regal
4. swim-skim-skip-ship-shop-stop

5. a. light
   b. Mexican
6. chandeleir (chandelier)
7. 1. hoe 2. woe
   3. foe 4. roe
   5. toe

LP-12

1. a. mess b. club
   c. jam d. crank
2. daydream
3. a. dueled
   b. brigade
4. rage-race-pace-pact-fact-fast-fist

5. a. Surrealism
   b. informal
6. transparant (transparent)
7. 1. shower 2. cower
   3. dower 4. empower
   5. tower

THINKATHON II

SCORESHEET

FOR TEAM_____

ACTIVITY   TOTAL POINTS SCORED

  I.   HYPOTHESIZING   _____

 II.   WHICH ONE DOES NOT BELONG?   _____

III.   MAKING COMPARISONS   _____

 IV.   TRIVIA   _____

  V.   MATH AND LOGIC QUIZ   _____

 VI.   LANGUAGE PUZZLERS   _____

            TOTAL TEAM SCORE   _____

This page should be duplicated for each team.

Certificate

This is to certify that

has participated in

THINKATHON 2

SEAL

Certificate Of Merit

This is to certify that

_____

was a member of the

Winning Team

THINKATHON 2

SEAL